Moor Poets

VOLUME II

A Collection of Contemporary Poetry from Dartmoor

Written by Moor Poets, a group of Dartmoor-based writers
Edited by Lucy Lepchani, Jennie Osborne,
Karen Eberhardt-Shelton and Caroline Wilson

Published by Moor Poets

This book is made possible with support from the Arts council England and
the Dartmoor National Park Authority

Published by Moor Poets,
Moor Poets, 23 Brooklands, Totnes, Devon TQ9 5AR, UK.
www.moorpoets.org.uk
Email: info@moorpoets.org.uk

Cover painting and design by Petra Tilly:
Petra@petratilly.co.uk

Typesetting: main text in Minion, cover and title page in Humana.

A catalogue record for this book is available from the British Library.

First printing November 2005

ISBN 0-9551114-04
ISBN 978-09551114-0-2

Printed by Moor Print in Manaton, Dartmoor, Devon, UK.
Email: moorprint@macunlimited.net

An Introduction to Moor Poets - Volume Two

Moor Poets started in spring 2003 and has gone from strength to strength ever since, with an ongoing programme of workshops in locations around the moor, which aim to encourage people of all ages and experiences to write. This includes workshops led by Caroline Wilson in Dartmoor Prison. We have been delighted with the enthusiastic response to Moor Poets Volume 1, which came out in July 2003, and hope that this second volume will also bring pleasure to many.

We, the editors, have truly enjoyed reading all 200 entries for the selection process. As well as bringing Dartmoor sharply alive in the mind's eye, both the poems that were selected and those that were not convey fresh interpretations of the place as we know it, and the ways in which people relate to it. We are particularly glad to include work by prisoners from Dartmoor Prison who participated in workshops held there during the year.

For many, the metaphor of landscape and its features were a vehicle for sharing joy and loss or for reflecting passionately on the issues of the wider world: environmental destruction, war, patriarchy, poverty, the arts, freedom and the daily round. There were also strong themes of Dartmoor's mysteries and secrets, surprises and comforts, faith, our ancestors and sacred space.

We hope that Moor Poets 2 will open a window onto the lives of some of the people who live, work and visit Dartmoor, and their relationship with the land and with Nature, and that readers will be inspired to visit these places for themselves and perhaps to write about them.

We would like to thank all those involved in the evolution of Moor Poets Vol.2: Matt Harvey, Alice Oswald, Peter Oswald, Susan Taylor, Chris Waters and Caroline Wilson, who led workshops, and the poets who have participated in them. Also, Penelope Shuttle and Clare Seal who assisted us in the final selection process; Petra Tilly for her evocative cover design and artwork, and Moor Print for once again producing a fine book.

We also thank our funders, Arts Council England, the Dartmoor National Park Authority, and Teignbridge and West Devon District councils, for their support and encouragement.

Most of all we are grateful to those without whom this book could not exist, all the poets who have shared their visions of Dartmoor with us.

November 2005

CONTENTS

page

Beating the Bounds

High walls
wet laurel
white doves
rain

Following well worn footpaths
I walk the green boundaries
of my heart

Over dripping hedges wild
with thorn and willow
an unreachable skyline

Nearby
the smell of wet tarmac
gardens glimpsed beyond stone walls
grey roofs and copper beech leaves

A dipper skimming the brown river
windflowers growing in rough grass
a continuum of birdsong
and running water

white doves
wet laurels
high walls
rain.

Bridget Thomasin

The Moor above Princetown, Dartmoor

The wood surprises with its green, mossed gloom
and stillness, bird chatter hushed in mist which
fleeces the knotted floor, mutes colour
with the breath of hidden streams.
Known features of the scene assume
new shapes, shapes shift, dissolve, fray
to fear's shadows flapping up from
vision's edge, dark wing beats creaking
warning prophecies, harsh voices
croaking their stern edicts on some
ancient law transgressed by our casual,
intruding gaze and clumsy tread.

Stark limbs rake the escaping light
where tree mass thins to moor's expanse.
Straining at the boundaries, a scaled oak
struggles in the ivy's coils, corded
in the slow constriction of its
sinuous embrace. We emerge to a
blurred perspective printed with the
crumbling script of an abandoned track
which once, scattering the browsing sheep,
unrolling echoes in the tunnel's throat,
clattered the blank-faced convict train
to Princetown Jail.

There, angled granite stamps a different creed
challenging tors' primitive authority,
yet crouches in the shadow of its stones
and storms. Wind still stalks the grey perimeter,
haunts the waste with its lament,
clangs shut the heavy door of penal solitude.

Helen Boyles

Houndtor

wears rain like a weapon
shakes the sky

till it sounds like a horn
from the underworld

scatters sheep
weaves the strangled cry of jackdaw

raven, buzzard
into a cloak

rides off with it
daring the clouds to race.

Miriam Darlington

Venford

At the reservoir, the Canada Geese
were all of one mind at the narrowest point,
forty of them, the water camouflaged

by the yellow spines of trees.
She was drawn to their impassive
white and black faces – the only sound

in the cool of the evening their beaks
dip-dipping at the surface.
At the sight of her, no bitter alarm,

but there was a division, the group
parted and headed away as if threaded on
one long piece of string. She stepped back,

and they began to reform with the occasional
low squashed honk of recognition.
Looking again, as she felt she must,

the two groups were no longer distinguishable,
returning with one body to her beginning.

Julie-ann Rowell

Susanna Petherick

"was enwraped and buried in a shroud of sheep's wool"
at Buckland-in-the-Moor, Sept 15 1727.

With snow cold hands she carries limp lambs
ears drooping like snowdrops
thaws them at the hearth till they have strength
to bleat for their mother's milk.

The spinning wheel hums in her bones
pulse beats to the rhythm of her sole
pressing the treadle that flies the wheel -
whirring, binding, twisting.
Hungry like a stream of water
wool thread pulls through the spindle
spirals between thumb and finger
wears down a groove in the skin.

Coffins cost more than a bundle of fleece -
she is wrapped in a winding sheet of cloud,
of dandelion clocks, old man's beard,
rosebay willowherb,
thistledown - spun ghost flowers -
the colour of morning light in a still pool
to fold her in the warm smell she loved
fresh wool, velvety new lambs.

Becky Gethin

Hoof Prints

My spade clunks against horse shoes:
rusted, thin at the toe:
relics of ghosts weigh heavy in my hand.

Wilfred recognised each horse's shoe -
first Darling, then Prince, and last of all
Charlie, retired when the first tractor arrived.

Work horses threaded through his life:
long after tractors had heated cabs
(too cushy, not real work, he said)
their booming tread still echoed in his bones.

Beneath whirling swallows his horse would pull
the wagon piled high with hay from first light
until darkness brought an end to work.

In spring the horse hauled
cart-loads of manure. Come winter,
logs were dragged through sucking mud
to keep the farm-house warm.

After each day's work, the tired horse
turned out to graze would upend himself,
roll from side to side, hooves flailing.

Standing four-square he would snort,
stretch his neck, shake his skin free
of the impress of collar, harness, load,
feeling wind sift sweated fur.

Iron-rimmed hooves once imprinted this land
with Wilfred, in mud-caked boots,
walking step by step beside them.

Becky Gethin

Change of Tide

Does just plain corruption burn in my lonely eyes
Or am I just a product of my own demise
For years my mind has ruled me, and set my path in life
A one way track of destruction, sabotage and strife.

I've never tried to change it, I've never had a clue
Give me half a chance and I'm sure I'll rob you too
Now I've never believed in anything, never had the chance
People say'here's Dexie, he'll rob you in a glance'.

So what has changed inside me? To give me such a chance?
A project set in Dartmoor is the start to my advance
An outer change, an attitude change, a heart change
But most of all an inner change.

Well now my heart is smiling, and my eyes are lonely no more
This jail course has saved me and thanks to the Father who I now adore.

D.B.

Ghost in Residence

I hit the ground running
and maybe the house had had enough
of the coming and going. An atmosphere
of leaves pawed over the light,
where wisteria insinuated
in through metal windows.

I put a mug down on a lurching chair
and spilt most of its contents
over my copy of *Dartmoor Visitor*.
The floor tilted there.
How come I'd forgotten this angle?

Wind rumbled in the chimney enclosure
like an irritable colon;
a remnant of the angry spirit
a distant neighbour sent packing,
as an uncalled favour.

I never laid eyes on that exorcist,
I'd asked just to fix a lock on the door.
A close neighbour told me,
he'd bragged he'd found
some butcher ghost by the cloam oven,
arms larded in blood.

Susan Taylor

The Song of the Moor

Ancestors: Listen poets, to the secrets we are shouting!
We are calling our dreams to the dreamers!
Revealing our stories to you, to you!

Big Stone: Hear me. This is the silence of the clinging of moss.
This is the sound of the resting of granite.
This is the song of twenty million years of being stone.

Ferns: Hear us from the deep green whispering tongues
That spread and span with symmetry's fronds
And lisp in subtle breezes and the tender cool of shade.

Ancestors: We have drummed our heartbeat across the years
That you might know us in your selves
And remember the songs of the cradling years,
The songs in your cells since the cradling years.

West Wind: For I have caressed and carried countless voices
Shaken their blossoming soft from the trees
Gathered their scent from summers passing
Spread them tenderly over your hills and spilled
The banks of rushing rain to weave the singing
silver streams.

Oak: Sturdily and steadfast, knowledge comes with
keeping still.

Ivy: And turning with the spiral year yet clinging tightly
where you will.

Elder: Be nourished by the harvests as they rise from every place.

Foxglove: Though sometimes death is hiding, sometimes
stares you in the face.

Stonecrop:	Like me, pierce all your dreams awake with
	floribunda stars
	Defy the power of struggle with the strength of roots
	held fast.

Stonecrop: Like me, pierce all your dreams awake with
                          floribunda stars
              Defy the power of struggle with the strength of roots
                          held fast.

Ancestors: For we are the earth, have always been
              Flesh rot to soil and bones to dust
              Yet our souls that dwell in the realm of song live on:
              In the stillness of granite and howl of the wind
              In the wingspan of buzzard, bright yellow of gorse,
              In your medicine plants and new wool from the flock:

              Our stories are scattered like seeds for the dreamers
              And poets that might know our rhythms,
              Ten thousand years turning.

Lucy Lepchani

Blackbird Dawn

When I wake from the dark,
bring me to this music
once again, this purling

song, trickling like a brook
through shadow, with sunlight
glancing off mottled rock.

Chris Waters

Moonbathing

Moon hurtles, full blown
triumphant through star-scattered sky,
scudding hill-tops as we follow
bootshod, footsure, clambering boulders,
picking the path beneath snaggle-twig branches
down by the snaky black river.

Light spangles in shimmers, embroiders in sheen,
stitching the high ground's hemline, silver
on the deep spread quilt of night.
Rising from stark, leaf-breathed hush
the silhouette of wing-spanned owl
spreads wide and beats the sudden air
and glides, to settle in silent shade
of woodland's tight drawn cloak.

Path becomes earth soft, dew-grassed.
A grove that knows our names, soon greets.
We stop and listen to rhythms within,
tasting the vapours of loam and sap
as Moon spills illusions of smithereen sequins
beneath the waters' soft quicksilver song

and opalescence floods, omnipotent,
stuns us and captures in gossamer nets
and snares awareness,
illuminates inside our skulls,
commands joyous high tides within the blood,
raises us cup-full like lunatic wine
to the cheer of traditions still weaving Her way
with a sacred and unbroken thread.

Imbibing the luminous languor of night,
absorbing, reflecting Her face,
we bare our bellies, breasts and limbs
to the silver-blue kiss of Moon's speaking-in-tongues
as Her blessing alights on our flesh.

Lucy Lepchani

Return

Fired in the kiln of centuries it bides its time
this watchful place
stores yesterday stone-deep

bone-deep

The sky is a shell singing my mother's songs
it hurts to hear them

haunts

I knew the words once   lived along to them
danced to their pulse
I am their stranger now   so long away

The moor is patient   lexicon landscape
waiting to teach me again.

Sheena Odle

We will Carry them Forever in our Scars

Here is raven scar my stories woven into blood
stories carved on living skin, threading new words into flesh
threading old words into new, old words into new
I mark the words so they will live, I do not let a story die
these things are scraped into me
I'll carry them forever, forever in my scars
I'll carry them forever, forever in my scars

this tale will be remembered, I work with needles of white bone
warm soot ground with fat and oils for ink to blacken my smooth bowl
with fire to make the story leap and beaten drums to pin it down
with spells to let the story breathe the magic of a frosted night
lull it into sleep once more
I'll carry it forever, forever in my scars
I'll carry it forever, forever in my scars

here is the truth so cut it deep, it can't be lost or thrown away
cut it deep so we shall know when drifting snows have changed its shape
truth has a beak that tears, truth has a ripping claw
it has a wing to lightly brush away the heavy dust of years
so the eyes may open wide
we'll carry it forever, forever in our scars
we'll carry it forever, forever in our scars

follow a trail the raven marked as words unravel from the skin
our land is there and all the sky and all the songs we ever heard
all the people we have taken with us as we travel on
every ghost with whom we've whispered far inside a notch of time
all the old hopes, all the new
we'll carry them forever, forever in our scars
we'll carry them forever, forever in our scars

all the land we ever loved, all the death we ever feared
all the truth we ever yearned for, all the songs we ever heard
we will carry them forever in our scars
we will carry them forever in our scars

pin them deep into our skin so we can make them last
in this way we will never lose our future and our past
we'll carry them forever, forever in our scars
we'll carry them forever, forever in our scars

Carolyn Hillyer

Groundswell

Today the plates are moving,
a fault at the heart of Dartmoor.
There should be tearing,
jagged edges, tectonic scrape.

Here, weary of autumn rains
the earth has bloated.
We balance on the riverbank,
feel the undulation,
watch the land vibrate.

Someone pokes a toe
through shivering grass:
the river oozes through.
We test our weight
as though stepping onto ice,
enjoy the ripple, the peaty gush.

Today, mainly unnoticed,
something shifted.

Lyn Browne

Farmer

Few envy me.
Up early out till late
weathering winter.
But few know
the joy of a dew-washed sky
fall of a moth-mist evening
a strutting pheasant's gleam over stubble.

I move with the cattle
see the lumbering sway of flank and belly
breathe their grassiness
hear a flurry of rising geese
the soft longing of sheep.
I start at a lark's sheer take-off
his sky piercing song.

The sky is awash with gulls
as red clay curls away
from my plough's blade
and furrows lead my eye
to where the field tips off
the lip of the hill
and the sea begins.

There's mud where cattle gather
the yard's aslop with slurry
but my eye holds distance
and wordless calls fill my ear.

Mel Lancaster

Moorland Tinner's House

Encrusted on its hollow,
A granite doorpost points the way up the coomb,
Staunchly standing proud of long-defeated walls
And broken lintel at its foot,
Half-submerged in reeds and grass.
These fragments, by a single rowan framed above,
Lie moated round by rippling spoil tips
Beneath a green tarpaulin moss,
Masked and uneroded.

This pillar part-described the frame through which
A tinner passed, a fulcrum balancing his worlds.
At evening, this stone would brace his back
As, hand in pocket, he would arch his spine or rub his belly.
It would fizz indignant when he flamed a lucifer across its grain,
While, through the smoke-licks, he thought back and forward
To adjacent daylight's drizzle-leadened tasks.

Feeling warmth behind,
He'd roll his face from withering breeze
Towards the inner glow and,
Stroking crystal flanks in pride and resignation,
Perhaps picked at a dark crack where a bloody bandaged
Hand had stained a hidden message in his DNA,
Stowed and undecoded.

Other clues are few now:
Beside the ford, no track
Beyond the sheep-worn shingle;
No scent besides the gorse.

Looking down, this lichen-spattered plinth
Suffices as a steadying prop for
Carefree hikers' glasses trained on other distant stones.
Only otherwise a lookout for a wheatear sentinel.

Paul Foster

16

Haytor Granite Tramway 1776-1858

Have you seen the tramlines up upon Haytor
Where once men quarried granite from beneath the moor
For 80 years and more, trucks loaded to the brim
Transported blocks of granite down to the River Teign.

From there, blocks travelled widely up and down the land
And men selected granite for the buildings they had planned
It was at this time in London, that the British Museum arose
And it was the Dartmoor granite that those workmen chose.

London Bridge was also built with granite strong and true
It stood across the River Thames from 1831 to 1962
This bridge was then transported to folk across the sea
And there in Arizona, a part of Dartmoor will always be.

When next you visit Exeter, a war memorial can be seen
With the Cathedral behind you, just stand upon the Green
There a tall imposing obelisk that reaches to the skies
Has names carved in granite of those who gave their lives.

Audrey Elphick

Gemstone

With joy-fed tears,
which well from eyes unseen
to flood the care-worn years,
the great gemmologist,
in cool grey night,
has shaped, transformed,
the spewed-up stone.

Through Okement, Dart,
Bovey, Tavy,
Taw, Tamar, Teign
and tributaries galore
the princely moorstone shines,
all timely cut and crystal glazed;
full-fingered, fetched
and set apart
from man's mundane designs.
Save where mine, pit
and storage lake
scratched out their hollow;
where track and road
rose up to follow.

Cott, homestead, forest,
farm and field took root
within the great reserve
and now sustain the ghosts
of men who lived
to the bleat of the sheep,
who moved to the lode
and bled the veins
of iron, copper, tin,
which lay within
Devon's granite gem.

Trevor Germon

18

Cawsand Hill

From Cawsand Hill I see
on an overcast February day

a shaft of sunlight
pierce the grey clouds

to play like a searchlight
on the fields below

making a smile in the weekend
of the friends from London
who came to stay.

They like to see Cawsand
once a month throughout the year,

clamber on its flanks
and search for the rainbow

that penetrates its purple heart
until it's time to go home.

Ron Mayers

The Eye

It's the first time we've found a water blister,
and we toe the centre – a wobble of spongy turf
sending a little geyser-burst of black water.
The river water is dog brown,
but the moor deep-down has coloured
this geyser black as tar; a dark eye pricked.
The day is all about being wet. Fir trees shower.
Rain finds gaps in our clothes, although no one
complains. Ground is saturated leaf mulch,
a squelch of loam. The river gorges a route.
Nameless river. Impossible to cross.
Hold hands at the edge because it's all teeth.
There is subsidence; the earth black
around the edges. I sway on the kilter,
but we continue along the tilting track.
If I find another blister I'll leave it intact;
something about tampering. I tread with care,
losing sight of my friends, who suddenly
seem so hurried. Thistles crowd, the river leaps;
the ground gives way.

Julie-ann Rowell

A Steady Stream of Words

Today, a lone fisherman stood in the embrace
of his beloved river, all her green wings and towers
folding him in the shawl of her watery hem
as he silently probed in the pools of a dream~
bluebells behind him as though sky had fallen
to the ground. Ah, I thought, the ways
of earth are very knowing, and the flowing
without parallel in any human scheme.

The rocks lying on the bottom like drowned furniture,
granite dishes rocking slowly in the wet push,
rugs laid down on sand, liquid chairs
and seats preserved under the lissom glide,
water duvets pulled over stony beds,

lulling them to sleep in swirlings and eddies
the sibilant whispers against
barriers, like dialogues of what is and why this,
what design puts down in iron putty,
mineral mud, the dark basement of certain depths
where all the rooms and stairs and hidden
crannies are purled over~
where acorns splash like tiny meteors
diving into depthless heaven.

All those elements swirl and deepen,
widen to a flat calm, then ripple white-crowned
in ceaseless murmurs past
faces blurred and bodies promised
to the steady mind of River, brought down
to the entry mouth of sea, the very world
opening to receive what began as tiny trickles born
on Dartmoor land where ponies wade and dribble.

Karen Eberhardt-Shelton

Teign In May

The beech leaves drop small stones into themselves,
Dip pale tongues to sip their memory from the river skin;
The air ticks under steady midday rain
Rinsing thoughts out of bluebells to hang between
The shelves of gold and grey.
Black wet silhouettes inside a cone of bowing leaves,
Nodding every drip that rolls into the heady flow;
The river slips below the long forgotten bridge,
Insubstantial space shrinking between white breath,
Sodden moss, slick stone.
There is a quiet heart grieving among all this noise,
Drinking at the edges of the tree's arms,
Lying looking up, pointing at its brethren high above;

Sadness presses its spoor by the glassy moat,
Its note, the pensive curl of a bulb of water,
Warming a pilgrimage down scalp and cold hair;
Abandoned light forgets clammy ferns,
Wet space reflects the streak of kingfisher,
Still boughs crying patterns onto the water's slow shoulders
Pocked with shadows and with dreams,
Skyless, some part of the world becomes a thousand years ago,
Slow time falling, interrupted, from grey to black.

Charlotte Jones

On my side of the river

On my side of the river we have new born foals

On my side of the river we have new born calves

On my side of the river we have baby birds

On my side of the river we have baby hawks

On my side of the river we have a family of woodpeckers

On my side of the river we have egg-snatchers

On my side of the river we have a leaning telephone box

On my side of the river we have a pole
delivering broadband

On my side of the river we have a bard delivering magic

On my side of the river we have a smith with an
enchanted hammer

On my side of the river we have an old woman with sparrows nesting
in her hair

On my side of the river we have an old man with
a badger's sett in his beard

On my side of the river we have a child whose voice is the river

On my side of the river his cradle floats in
the eddies

A traditional 'flyting' poem by **Pat Fleming** *and* **Simon Williams**

23

Lost Beyond

Lost beyond the weed encrusted pond
stagnant. Deep and still and dangerous
revealing only indigo beneath thin shards of light
that hover on the margins. Never. Nothing.
Mill pond, absolutely still.
No old stone impounds the rise and fall
of what was once the stream
now a torrent leaps and rolls and burgeons
boulders in its path oozing squelch at the water's edge.
Buckets of excess, too much
too dangerous, abundant, fearful:
not now, not yet death
life before death, life first
and flourishing, life slithering between the weeds
brown trout and vivid worm
flattened, rendered null in the fullness of the flood.
Mrs Noah wonders if the grain will last
while the men discuss the meaning of meaning
and its valid interpretation
buckets of shit unemptied at their feet.
Late now. Too late. The fire has started
and the bombs have fallen
foul into the desert's cool embrace
all heat and heart congealed in the blood of others
and their children's children.
Deliver us from the misdeeds of our fathers
and our chidren from our own.
Stone at the water's edge, a pebble
no longer shining on the bare earth.

Susannah Lash

Lost

We are lost in grave mist,
a stream is a voice
beckoning, *this way, this way,*
though you remind me:
never follow water to its conclusion –
listen for the giggle of a cattle grid
leading through the green heather.

Our compass has betrayed us
on the downward slope.
My feet are swollen against
the rigid leather of the boot.
The boggy ground sucks.

If we could but lie still,
catch our breath,
be made love to by the cold,
feel it creeping up our legs
to be found coiled together
amongst the gorse.

Julie-ann Rowell

Lost

I am like a summer's child in a land of snow
And who knows what the future holds
For tomorrow never knows
I'm lost in a land where the cold wind blows

I could have strolled through sunshine
Through valleys and glades
The decision was mine
Yet I chose to lie in the shade

I'm down in the doldrums with no wind in my sails
I'm alienated and estranged
I'm just another prisoner in an over-crowded jail
Just waiting for the winds of change

I feel like a passenger on a runaway train
Too nervous to apply the brakes
If I could live my life again
Would I still make the same mistakes?

I'm wandering down the road that I chose
Lost in a land where the cold wind blows.

M.M.

The Way Through

There have been a million obstacles in my way today, or so it seems;
The scramble in the foetid darkness of the loft
Trying to find my paints,
The wasp attacking me in the garden,
The fear of not knowing who will be there
What will we do? How will it be?

Tramping up the path, not knowing
What to write
What to draw.
The gates, several of them,
Metaphorical brick walls to my journey.
The stream, overblown with rains' swell
Forming a deep gushing chasm
Requiring a leap of faith onto the one submerged stepping stone.
Losing the path, tearing my clothes on brambles
Battling through the heather
Sweat running down my back.

Obstacles, barriers, trials.
But I did keep going
My mood lifting into brightness
With the path to the tor.

And if it had not been for the cruel gorse, the stream, the rusty gates, the
angry wasp
I would not have seen
The velvet-winged butterfly
The white plume of water
The flowers hidden in the grass.

I would not have felt the mystery of the silent deep pool
The joy of the beauty of the day
The elation at my first print
The cleansing gush of words on the page.

And perhaps now, at the end of the day
The wasp has lost its sting
And perhaps I have too.

Claire Hardisty

If This Poem...

If this poem were an owl, it would be all
seeing, all knowing, like the branch on which
it's sat, knowledge upon knowledge, an understanding
of growth, life and the wings in which it is
carried.

If this poem were a wall, some people would
be talking to it, some people would be climbing it,
some would smash it, some would paint it,
and usually live within one.
But it still remains just a wall.

If this poem were a wish, I would turn
it into three, one for the past, one for now,
and one for the future to be, as of before, as
of now, I can see, but the future one is
left up to me.

R.C.

I Search for Summer

I search for summer

in this place
walking, walking down,
my raincoat dripping,

hear trees shake
fat drops of rain into drowned moss,
see the river slide like a crocodile over rock,

snarl a heron's scarecrow legs
in ribbons of water,
taste river-tang in my throat,

sense otter among
black oak ribs,
watch biblical clouds split the sun,

tip the valley into amber velvet;
and when I am the last,
the very last person alive,

a sudden bog
swallows my welly,
eats my sock,

laughs at me, bare toes flapping.

Miriam Darlington

My Blue Heaven

Above Bonehill, a sky of liquid blue,
A yellow kite that bobs and floats and strains
Beyond, dark hump of Hameldown
Soon to be blotted out by mist and rains.
People like pins atop the cushioned rocks
Seem joined by string to cars below
So when a cold wind blows, and skies begin to frown
It tugs them back to town.

The cows are coming home across the moor
Out of the slanted light
Through imperial heather, golden gorse
They've grazed the day away and step out sure
Towards a peaceful night.

Is home then upalong or outalong?

Is heaven a departure over sea or plain
Reached through a tunnel on a celestial train
By shadowed valley, gated dwelling place?
Not 'over there', though hidden now from view,
Nor even skywards, cheating clouds and space,
Not going away into a distant blue,
More, after death's concussion, a return, head clearing,
Coming to.

Ann Stone

Enclosure

The wind has come back:
there is a passion in wind
better than still air,
better than the cloying grey of mist
that lies thickly in the dip
between the hills. A wild goose
bells like a hound
over the roof to the pond.
Dark trees bend and crack,
whip back. There is nothing human
in this landscape, only cattle
edging each other out of the ring-feeder,
watched by crows.

In this solid house
we silently suffer winter,
create fires, imitate living.
Sunk in granite we have no fear
of hurricane or flood:
only the stealthy creep of radon,
the thrust of storms eroding
earth from stone, creating gullies
forming waterways
from newly pushed-up springs.

Caged, we wait for sun,
for the freedom from enclosure,
the flinging open of windows,
the jubilant, daring, crass
rejuvenation of spring.

Jane Beeson

A Poetry Workshop in Dartmoor Prison

We gather in a snug cell
Ann and me and you eight
men with your gentle eyes
and hands that write poems.
We play with rhythm and rhyme
images of a proud tiger
caged lion and a kitten
cosy in front of the fire.

Grey in here
   bright out there.

You write of lost loves and loves
you hope you have not lost
of longings for the smell of bacon
and just ripe Camembert
of night skies in the South Seas
of primroses in Welsh valleys
of missing little Emma and Jack.

It's good
   and then its over.

We say goodbye. Keys clank
in locks. Ann and I walk back
between huge granite walls
fences topped with razor wires
and old rags like freedom flags.
Wind whistles. More keys

in doors and gates

and out
    into the car park

where a prisoner
soon to be released
pulls weeds, very slowly.

Caroline Wilson

Walls

Walls can be built to keep prisoners confined or keep people out.
Walls can be 20 foot high to separate Catholics and Protestants
and keep them from attacking each other.
Walls can be built to surround Palestinians and make them prisoners
in their homeland.
Walls can keep you away from danger.
Walls can be dry stone and can roam for miles along the rolling hills.
Walls can be a plaything for children to balance along and walk tall.
Walls can make you think of cliffs, housing estates, prisons.
Or walls can also make you think of ice cream.

M.M.

Land Lord

Grey, night-specked
and carbon-fibre hard,
the giant Land Lord lies
bedded in grave
moorishness.

He time defies,
and all release denies.

Whip-lashed, washed,
beset by west-born winds:
softened, scoured and striped
by stripling streams;
pocked with sucking mires,
by druids dressed in circling dreams
and rows convoking old desires;
the cooled melt is massed
in bold terrain.
This Dart-split moor
is his domain.

Bewitched by mists;
diced and devilled
by dagger frost;
grilled and seared
by all seeing sun;
hounded by Black Dogs;
the quarry
of marauding
mason ghosts;
he locks the past away
and rests content.

His rights hold fast;
time pays the rent.

Trevor Germon

Snakes

With a rattle of shale
the ivy comes away
spilling its secret
down the quarry face.

A mandrake would have shrieked.
Slipping from the crack
a tangle of snakes
slides into the light
sleekly unravels
frantic to seek
a darker space.

No trace of struggle,
only a brief gleam,
a hint of circles sketched on air
a film of dust now settling
on glossy leaves.

Lyn Browne

Cat Elegy

Enid brought her to us
when Tom was barely born,
found her down by the Torridge
in a sack, old sack.

A familiar cat, from a piebald mother
and an old tom strong
from the scraps of the village
and black, jet black.

They say that cats love places;
warm roofs, hot stoves.
You must rub their feet in butter,
to distract them when you move,

but this one took to people –
never wandered more than metres.
She was happy with her household,
had nothing else to prove.

Tom has gone to college
and still the cat has work to do,
soaking up the sun
on the cobbles in July.

As her fur barely rises;
breathing light, heart faint,
another summer drains away.
She's lost a final ally.

Tonight, beneath a feline moon,
I slide the earth by shovelful.
The metal spade-shaft rings
like an old church bell

and the pile of soil I've dug,
fits exactly in the hole,
like the old cat had no volume
after one remembered spell.

Simon Williams

Behold the Morris!

Eighty degrees and still
not noon over the regimented
grass, close mown without spirit
or clover or daisy – a perfect order
to march for the red brick and hollyhocks,
for the broad door, highly glossed,
bluer than the sky, with polish and
more polish on the oh so bright brass.
The slender spire looks back, inverted
and bulbous now, beyond the chestnut
spread broad, spread deeper
than the cliché, where shaded we lay
between dances, between the ash sticks beating,
the tatters flying, between the rags ripped
from the peaty soil, from the rough granite,
between the ribbons, between the bells.
Behind the lenses,
focus, click, print:
Timeless.

Anthony Golding-Cook

Heavy Horses

The heavy horses float
weightless through long grass,
fluidly streaming,
each huge fringed hoof
placed delicately.
The grassy fronds
spring back as they pass.

Rumps ripple with
slow muscle, backs sway,
manes lift and flop softly.
Weight bows
their huge heads,
but slowly lifting,
liquid eyes focus
on the right spot
for the next step.

Around them the invisible yoke,
the chains, the shafts for
pulling plough, cart or wagon.
They pull against the heavy air
missing the old resistance
missing the need to strain.

Mel Lancaster

Migrant

Walking, we come across
deserted stone-rows:

here are ground-lines,
walled shelter-shapes

of roughed granite stacked
shin-high, nudged together,

penned in a huddle, soft
with sprung grass and brackens,

stone-shields of lintel and jamb,
hearth and doorway,

squared against moorland
rain-blast and cloud-blow:

silenced, we turn homeward,
and a migrant wind, on an in-breath,
shifts through the ferns.

Chris Waters

A Curtain Across the Dark

A dark doorway
            into a little silence

swallows fly through my fingers

the breath of their swooping glide
across the threshold
disturbs my shadow.

A little silence
a dark doorway
a block of shadow
          dust
             straw
a line of words
            to be stepped over
and seen from the other side.

The threshold changes

a lichen covered thorn tree

the shadow of a rock
on sunburnt grass

a song's refrain.

Swallows always find
the dark doorway
but sometimes I step past
missing the shadow of silence
the otherside of the song.

Dusty light   a curtain
                    across the dark
light I can touch
            play with
hold out in my hands
                    to the swallows.

Bridget Thomasin

When Everything's been Said

Watching water
heron grey and still
just for a moment
when everything's been said
rocks remember sunlight
the substance of a river bed
changing colour
under running water.

Bridget Thomasin

Wild Water

The Tavy cascades over mossy boulders
Unstoppable from the high moors,
Thunders, accelerates, foams, churns,
Gurgles and rushes over rapids,
To sparkle like crystal in sun.

I stand beside the stream
The sound drums out everything
Washes my mind clean.

Clare Masters

Sighting

If you're lucky, you may see one cut through the clouds.
It's possible in winter, when the air
crackles with a deep hoar frost
or a dry sugaring of snow,
but never after rain.

You may mistake it for a low-lurking sun, scarfed in haze,
as it hangs, pulsing amber, above the rockline.
Watch as it sweeps its wings back
like an arrowhead at rest,
catches a current, somersaults
on the edge of belief.

Jennie Osborne

Bluebells beneath Hound Tor

Dew, half-dried, balances on that blade
where longing is gathered in to itself
and held for a moment, before opening
winged hands and letting the air take it up.
Even then, does something hold back?
Something lighter than the top spray of
a wave, the part that might never fall
back down to sea, something that is
almost nothing but not quite – hovering
in the gesture between sky and earth,
a thing so small that may have heard
just then (   ) the sound
of a million or a million or more million
flowers opening.

Jo Marie

Field

Stooping to inspect
furrows
in his stone-walled
field
in long evening
light,
a man and his shadow
seem companionably
hinged.

Chris Waters

Blue from Blue

On a day of blue breezes, mistakenly,
Arrows fall short
Through a half-open window, stubbing
Cold glass; a stuffy curtain billowing,
Two newly-fledged swallows in my living room
Soft-land
And I take one and then the other in each hand.

Quietly they lie, broken pieces of the sky,
Beaks gaping like fish in a dead indoor space,
Wings swept and folded
Back, polished butterfly blues,
Heads perfectly round, holding a compass
Of all the airy latitudes,
Eyes dark globes, reflecting Devon's tilted views.

This moment, which will not repeat in my lifetime,
Is for them the greatest danger,
More than the Sahara, the Congo, sticky bird-lime.
I judge their weights, less than an ounce,
And toss them clear of man's harm, cat's pounce
To loop and swing on a string through summer skies
Until dry apple leaves lift and fall,
The dropping sun's angle is right,
And the air spins with dust and seeds which call
Them to Africa.

Thrumming and whirring, powerful engines
Fuelled by flies,
They disappear into the dark cloud with the gold rim
Which shapes and mends itself
In the winds blowing endlessly; trim
For their six thousand miles.

Landlocked, we emerge blinking, one day
In a distant April, when the blossom's on the plum,
Scanning a washed sky for the small blue darts, crying
"Here they come!"

Ann Stone

Blown Seeds

This is the signal of summer's end,
The season of blown seed.
They drift through my bathroom skylight,
macles on the white porcelain.
They lie like scattered oatmeal
among my kitchen crumbs.
Pinhead discs of gold
bordered with gossamer vanes,
they diaper every surface.
What they are I do not know
but, dozing in the garden afternoon,
I wake to find my forearm freckled with them.
Bury me in the churchyard now,
who knows what wildflower
I might rise come Easter.

Mary Morton

In the Woods

I saw four foals, the woman said,
while walking through the wood.
They're placid in the June sun –
don't seem so wild.
The Chinese ones.
Perhaps I misheard.

I saw four moles, she said.
Big paws like goalkeepers,
runnels in the leaf-litter,
mounds from coming up for air.
Blind as bats, but no wings.
Chinese moles?
I saw four Poles, she said,
The gentlemen of Warsaw, Kracow,
wander in the woods at Hembury.
Pickled beetroot at the ready,
stereotypes ticking from
the Chinese takeaways of Gdansk.

I saw four rolls – the baps, the baps,
four bowls the bodgers turned.
I saw four goals – 'Good shooting, chaps!',
four holes the Diggers churned.

Four doles
Four knowles
Four souls
There's little limit to the rhyme

Four tolls
Four voles
Four trolls
long hair, glass eyes,
arms out, grinning all the time.

In the end, there's no answer,
no chance to ask for a repeat.

Essential facts:
- There were four.
- They were Chinese.
- They were in the wood.
- They were worth seeing.

Simon Williams

Feathers

Of all the wonders ever heard
Consider the clothing of a bird;
Of all the qualities in a feather
Waterproof and warm against the weather,
Sustaining birds on wing in flight
Of multi-colours and black and white.
Proud fan-tailed peacocks in display,
Bright as rainbows, attract hens their way.
Their patterns act as camouflage
Hide hens on eggs at the sitting stage
Blend them in the natural surround
In trees, undergrowth or on the ground.
Feathers, almost weightless, range from long and strong
To fluff and down which cosies the young.
It's magical how birds are blessed
Compared to how we are, undressed.

Hubert Snowdon

Conversation

Tree: I lean, lean against the wind
as I have leaned since my once-pliant limbs
were fixed and frozen in this twisted state.

Wind: Ooh, ooh, there is no malice in my bite.
When I prevail, I may be strong
but wet and westerly.

Wall: Bend to the wind ? Not I !
I stand here strong as any standing stone.
Man-made, but made to last, crevice fitting crack,
weight balanced on wide base.
Tumble a little, I may,
but my heart is firm, based on the moor's strength.

Fern: Ah, the moor's strength, our home and nourishment.
Rich, peaty sludge feeds hairy stems and outstretched
fronds
fingering the rising mist.

Moss: But who supports you all ?
I matt your stones with my close pile,
knit them together, lest the wall may fall,
accept the seeds of foxglove and violet,
pennywort and stonecrop,
embrace them in my moist fecundity.

Tree: I long to stretch my lichened limbs
but rooted in this wall, my feet are shackled.

Wind: Ooh, ooh, blame me,
but I am in the nature of things
and in my own nature I can only blow and bend
but not to my will.

48

Barbed-wire:	Tut-tut. Cut-cut.
	Metal rules, poor fools.
	I care nothing for wind.
	Rustless, I defy rain,
	keep stupid sheep from climbing this wall,
	deter destructive humans from trampling
	and gathering you frothy flowers and fronds.
Road:	So right my friend.
	I am a metalled road and will last and last
	till time's end.
	Yes, we rule the moors my friend.
Wall)	Oh, so you say.
Wind)	But when the world has gone to pot
and Rain)	We'll be here, but you'll not !

Mel Lancaster

Spiralling Light

My lonely decline into drug abuse
has took its toll, my mind's abused.
Revolving doors that never stop!
Once in it's like a lock.
Round and round for years you go,
never to stop, always to flow.

So at what point do you stop and learn?
Put down your feet and try and turn?
The pathway is there all ragged and torn.
Pick the path up but let you be warned!
It may seem bleak and a dark cloud overshadow your way!!
But just keep walking – this is your day.

D.B.

Moor Or Less

You drag your chairs and tables to my waters
Desiccating bracken in your haste
Your shortcuts scourge new wounds into my torso
Careless feet delete my mossy face

I watch you as you scrawl upon my canvas
Your metal pens an ink clot in my veins
Seeping onto fauna and the flowers
Marking out my fields to play your games

Holes burn in my carpet from your thoughtlessness
My creatures rack upon your smoking coals
Lured closer to your feeding hand from interest
Then slaughtered on the road by four by fours

My body is a lay-by from your lifestyle
A welcome break from daytime ways and woes
You pull away recharged from flattened landscape
Exhausted from your fumes I watch you go

Nels Rodwell

Winter Sleep

Cover me with orange leaves and leave me
to unlace the seam of oblivion
and fall into slumber.
Rain-sheltered, spiralled in a russet bed,
folded in amber flakes:
fallen glories with memories of sky-blue.

Never to waken, let me be
the shade that eclipses the dark,
the sleep that paints no dreams,
the calm that feels only itself:
more than nothing, less than something

never to waken

until

The new light comes shining,
sharp enough to quicken me,
whose dawn-songs can blow apart my quilt
and lead me over leat and clitter
to hear the peals of a kinder copse,
breathe the edge of warmer breezes,
wear the sun-kiss on my brow:
to be more than something, part of all.

Paul Foster

I Don't Know When . . .

. . . the snow began
to fall,
down
from the faded denim sky,
pausing on the branches,
parting the pine needles,
plunging to the deeper darkness,
but,
I saw the dry brown burdock
become a cotton blossom
ripe for plucking,
ready for weaving into fine cloth
fit for a princess,
and
I felt the icy warm caress
upon my cheek,
the moisture pause on my lips
until
a myriad of sparkling flakes,
a million stars
burst forth as
a chorus
within me.

Helen Shelswell

Walking the Year

Today, bundled like Christmas parcels,
we walk the white moor,
flirt with the treachery of frost underfoot,
the frown of snow above the next tor,
with the chance we can't quite dismiss
of whitedown, drowning senses,
the world blinked out.

It doesn't happen. Instead,
watching our boot toes pick their way
through gorse and bracken,
we stumble, almost,
into an ice-picture, feathered in frost,
brittle over a pocket of air.

We stare a while, the damp of snow
creeping through our soles, until
one of us bends down, breaks it.
Splinters cascade from her hands,
the year's cargo of deaths and meetings,
its grazed shins and its music-making
seeping into soil.
She wanted to, she says, she really wanted to.

Jennie Osborne

Boxing Day Afternoon.

On Boxing Day we drove up to the moors
to find the snow near-gone, though trapped in ruts.
The sheep stood looking mournful in the cold
for it was sharp and crisp that afternoon.
No ponies could be seen, where usually
they form a cluster near the bridge at Shaugh
in hope of meeting generous human friends.

We left the car and walked towards the Plym:
fast-flowing water leapt with joyous splash
to overcome the boulders in its path.
Perhaps it was too cold to venture in
for one small dog who stood his ground to bark
ferocious protests to the river bank.
Nearby, the outspread arms of leafless trees
stood sentinel to form a silhouette
which cast a sense of calm security.
A place to pray in peace: I would have stayed
without distraction of the others there.

Once back inside the car and heading home
I looked towards an ever-changing sky
with no clear definition, just a blend
of colours which no painter could have planned.

Light grey, like smoke, soon wafted into pink
and then to languid lines of lavender
to lie upon a bed of cobalt-blue
that darkened slightly at the bottom edge;
and from this lower rim the sun escaped
to shine down on the water in the Sound
and make it glisten gold. It was surreal.

June Drake

Winter Evening

Barbed branches fingering an opal sky
and light listing to the west and
one bright star, singing down the years

what purity of tone in the cold air

in the cold air your words shape-shift
(I cannot speak)
curl into questions
(I have no answers)

disappear

this is an old land
I had forgotten how it feels

tides surge through the sentient stones

a white moon rises.

Sheena Odle

The Tavy in January

Today
no murmured river song
from a gently tumbling Tavy
today
an elemental roar of rage
constant and fortissimo
heavy with moorland mud
the water surges seaward
surfaced with off-white breakers
criss-crossing clashing
falling over themselves
venting wild fury on
freedom-restraining banks
today
is not a day for solace-seekers
this temperamental Tavy
carries murder in its swell

Jacqui Fogwill

Winter Birch

I lean on the slope
of the moor

leech the sky
with black veins

feel the shiver
of the earth

draw my bark close
taut as whale bone;

moth wisp peels
from my skin.

I see mortals pass
light as paper lanterns;

I am welded
to the granite

garlanded
with last leaf-fall.

I watch prayers
lift into the ether;

a blur of rain
folds over my skeleton

and lit with the morning,
sap pearls my buds

waiting, waiting
for the spring.

Miriam Darlington

Mind

The mind is a herd of cows

on a dull grey afternoon   suddenly finding itself

standing in a circle   all facing inwards

wondering what it is   supposed to be looking at

in the space in the centre

then

scattering

in

panic

Peter Brissenden

Don Quixote on Dartmoor

Prologue
I thought I saw the shade of Don Quixote
With lance of stars and cape of sunset red;
And behind him came a maid with Don Quixote
Who countered the outrageous things he said.

The Interlude
There's the monster of a whale on the wild, green shore
That's big enough to swallow sixty Jonahs---maybe more.
    No, no Don Quixote! That is Combeshead Tor
    Not rising from the seashore but the wild, green moor.

Dulcinea del Toboso, the lady I adore,
Is watching from her castle as she did in days of yore.
    No, no Don Quixote! I must set you right once more:
    It's just a sheep that's grazing on the top of Leather Tor.

In the valley there's an ocean that I've never seen before
Where high-built Spanish galleons go, and scores of cannons roar.
    No, no Don Quixote! They are not men o'war,
    But wild ducks in a thunderstorm on the lake at Burrator.

I see the dread enchanter no knight-errant can ignore,
And my lance is at the ready to strike him to the floor.
    No, no Don Quixote! Who'll believe you anymore?
    It's the television mast you see beyond the slopes of Cramber Tor.

The world it keeps on turning and it goes from bad to worse;
And Honour is a poem no more, but just a doggerel verse.
    Dear, dear Don Quixote, you are mad as mad it's true,
    But the world might be a better place if we were all as mad as you.

Epilogue
And then I saw the shade of Don Quixote
Ride through the night beside the silver streams;
And then, I think, the maid with Don Quixote
Became the Dulcinea of his dreams.

Edward Murch

A Place of Beauty

A vast exposure, wild desolate scrub land, granite tors;
The prison stands, monument to these long past wars.
Throughout the year and weather changes,
Nature assured it received the ranges.
The sheep they flourish, the ponies grow
A meagre subsistence when covered in snow,
But beyond all this its beauty abounds.
Celtic warriors who've long gone
Have left us memories, strange stone rounds.
The Bishops Way and the clapper bridges,
The 'moor' yields up history be it rounds or ridges.
To the unseen eye there are treasures to behold.
Autumnal colours are but a few for us to enfold.
Winter brings snow its blanket to cover.
There are many such stories still untold.
Though as time moves on and the earth grows cold
Spring comes forth, the circle of life can now remould.

D.P.

Warren House

I have found peace at this inn
   On sombre afternoons
When lamps were lit, and the dark
      came down,
I have found peace when the bracken
     was brown,
   On sombre afternoons.

And the talk with my friends was good
     in the twilight,
The hours were buttered with toast, and the
     jam was sweet.
The room flickered with flame; and the
     smell of peat
Brought peace to the stuttering firelight
   On sombre afternoons.

And the moor could rage its gorse and
     heather;
The mist swirl down; and wind and storm
Assail the fabric with their weather;
But still within the inn was warm
Of word and wit and wainscot light,
   Against the coming of the night.

I have found peace at this inn
   On sombre afternoons
When the lamps were lit, and the bracken
     was brown;
I have found peace when the dark came down
   On sombre afternoons.

Edward Murch

It's a Spring Thing

Is that you peeking round the mud
your sticky sap oozing up ?
Is this you causing such a clatter and rush ?
Everything out there shouting, posing, preening.
Other things pushing, bulging, splitting
spitting out a miracle or three,
disguised as soft curled ears,
green elf tongues,
and some prehistoric being from below.

Good morning to your chaos chorus,
to your dumb-striking beauty
going wondrous crazy all around.
No modesty or shyness here
once the first peep is out.
Joyous strutting
joins the fast food fandango,
everything wants to eat
everything else
then is eaten itself.

Good morning Spring
I hope my soul can join in uninvited…
this irresistible exuberance
from the footed and the rooted
the wingers and the swimmers..
'cos here I am
a hoppin' and a skippin' and a raising hallelujah
dancing up a loveliness
in partnership with you,
wanting you to eat me whole.

Cathy McGavin

Game of Life

The high hard line of moor intensifies -
darkness crouches over a valley mist

cattle graze a cold shoulder
return through the tied-open gate

fields both beckon and repulse -
a dog's bark jerks from the valley

moor's mass rebuffs, its peace eludes.
Where should I go for friendship

but down with the dog -
a hillscape alone is a lonely place.

I hear a sheep's cry, find a deserted lamb
caught in a rift that reaches sky.

Small birds pass from clump to clump
a crow carks with the metallic voice of a survivor

I love, I love, I am not severed as easily
as a scythe slides through grass

I am here with land, shall die in its keeping.

A wall's face rears in front of me
with the fine permanence

of rock embedded in mortar -
my feet find no footholds
I cling with the insistence of lichen
or canker growing on a rotting tree -

I will not slither unheard
like dried moss from roof to grass

but hang like an icicle
waiting on sun for freedom.

Jane Beeson

The Cuckoo's Voice is Insistent

As the girl's behind the till
Ballooning plastic bags
Battering the bell for a helper
My mind drifts…

A dark doorway silhouettes doves –
Jackdaws encroach along the barn face
Occupying each niche like a beach hut

Dandelions flock, yellow as a coward's heart
Transparent stems ooze whiteness
Gum fingers black

Cattle nose amongst them
Tearing at ground that stretches belief
In six weeks to mowing

The field narrows, mounts –
Sun dazzles off windscreens
Beetling over distant hills

Magnetised
My eyes argue with earth's turn
The deception, the trickery of spin

I look for a ball
Orange and spiked
Child art in a sky of post-card blue

On a rock I watch. Wait.
Through red-edged fingers sun burns lower
Red, red, red, white hot

Cows come round, scrape chins on granite
Blow cowy breath, gaze at me enshrined
Wander off to graze

One stays behind, the white of her eye
A quarter moon floating between Mars and Venus
In a vacant sky…

A helper brings the replaced item
 - my bill snakes out –
I grasp the wilful trolley
Steer it crab-wise for the exit.

Jane Beeson

Reprieve

The pebbles lap the last of weary water
The slack streams cannot slake their shrunken throats
An insistent sun saps strength from hissing grasses
Beside the banks burn brackens burnished fronds
The hillside bears its purple blaze of heather
The air
Too hot
Rolls over and is still
Sheep un-shorn sleep panting worn beside the tarmac shimmer
Reprieve beneath the shadows of the walls

Nels Rodwell

I am not My Name

Bowling up the long, green lane that leads to the Grey Wethers
The September ease dreaming its way through my hair –
A sudden pungent mottle of fungi…

Stopping to scrawl these lines - one by one as they come

A red admiral flies encircled by cones
And a brown dab of sepia linnet smudges the sky with its song

Distant gunfire almost spoils my reverie,
But the ancient moor ever bends its will
Towards the warrior.

I am drawn to ponder those men who have walked this road before me –
The miner, the murderer, the poet, the priest…
I am no longer foolish enough to think
I am anyone,
Nor that I was any of these, or could be again -
I am not my name.

There are only these two striding legs hurling me on,
And my thoughts - fleeting as the mossy webs
That stitch together these pines.

I reach the threshold of the moor,
Drop my baggage and leap down from a high wall
Onto the moor
And words are instantly swallowed by its fathoms.

Quiet for some time now…as thoughts begin to settle
And the poem enters deeper into my blood.

Twin circles of stone. Beautiful.
A moorland stream – I find myself naked, submerged in peat.
A dragonfly.

Drying in a warm autumn wind lying atop an ancient clapper bridge.

Homewards via Manaton –
A stream and an oak wood
With a copper-haired artist in it –
His easel supporting my day

A dreampool netted in beechleaves
Deep, Cold, Pure.

Trickling water – I follow – A spring.
I pull away mud, deadwood, leaves,
To reveal an opening under a rock - a quartz citadel.
Flowers – lilac and yellow
Today is my birthday.

A blessing and a prayer.

Richard Rudd

High over Hay Tor

You're miles and miles away
high over Hay Tor
flying north to Black Hill

soaring, then gliding
on long lazy wings
tumbling with ravens

humming your last songs
to the florescent gorse
to the soft-footed foals

chuckling as you leave
a chorus of skylarks
calling you up

smiling your broad smile
clouds drizzle your face
wash off the last crumbs of earth

brilliant spring sunlight
sharpens each rock below
turns each pool to shivering gold

*(for Steve Risley, a musician who loved Hay Tor,
and who died in April 2005, aged 50.)*

Pat Fleming